Connecting with God's Love

A Workbook
For Creative Object Lessons

Dennis M. Berkesch

Concordia Publishing House

Copyright © 2002 by Creative Communications for the Parish, Fenton, MO

This edition published by Concordia Publishing House
3558 S. Jefferson Avenue
St. Louis, Missouri 63118-3968
(314) 268-1000

Printed in the USA.

Purchasers of this publication may reproduce designs for the completion of the projects.

All rights reserved. Except as noted above, no part of this publication may be reproduced in any form without permission from Creative Communications for the Parish.

CONTENTS

A NOTE TO PASTORS, TEACHERS AND WORSHIP LEADERS   5

AN ALPHABET OF TEACHING HELPS   7

LABORS OF LOVE Occupations   15

STATES AND THEIR NICKNAMES   21

    State cards   28

SIGNS FOR OUR TIMES (Road Signs)   35

    Road Signs   39

CHRISTIAN SYMBOLS   40

WHAT'S IN A NAME?   50

    Name certificate   59

A CHURCH TOUR   60

TOOL BOX   64

HIKING WITH THE PSALMS   66

    Map   71

Note to Pastors, Teachers and Worship Leaders

Reminders of our loving God are all around us. Using objects and signs that we see every day and connecting them to biblical truths is one way to help children understand sometimes complex ideas. This book offers eight different series of object lessons for creative pastors, teachers, or children's ministry leaders to do just that. Suggestions for creative thinking and effective communication introduce ten-week, twenty-week, and even several yearlong series of object lessons. Object lessons presented in series form give children continuity, build anticipation, and invite them to return the next week.

With a workbook format, each series is built around a theme and offers leaders a Scripture verse, a thought starter, a visual aid or a take-home idea for each lesson. There's room for leaders to make notes, to expand on the basic ideas and to use their own imaginations and personal styles.

The small pictographs accompanying most of the lessons can be enlarged and used as visual aids in the presentations. Presenters are free to copy them for use as handouts in any of a variety of ways, or the images may spark imaginations for more concrete visuals with costumes or props.

What do a picnic table, sandpaper, or the Big Sky state of Montana have to do with the Gospel? Quite a bit, actually, when presented in the context of these object lessons. The variety is wide-ranging, but one purpose unites them all: sharing with the children of your congregation God's great love for us in Jesus.

An ALPHABET of Teaching Helps

SHARING THE GOSPEL WITH CHILDREN

A

Affirmation. In our presentations we often ask questions that encourage our young people to share their ideas. Saying "No, that's not right" may send a negative message and discourage participation in the future. Here are three positive responses that will affirm their participation:

   1. If the answer is on the right track, we can encourage further answers building on what was shared. We might say something like "It does start with that letter" or "O.K., what would come next after that?"
   2. If the answer would be appropriate in a moment or so in response to another question, we may ask them to remember what they said and promise to ask them to share it again.
   3. If the answer is not helpful, we can respond with "That's not quite what I was thinking."

By affirming their ideas we build relationships and encourage participation and openness.

B

Blueprint. Our teachers taught us to outline before writing research papers. Once we begin that practice, the quality of our papers improves. Working week to week on object lessons necessitates starting over with a search each week. How helpful it is instead to have a plan that will extend over a period of weeks or months. Knowing the lesson ahead of time gives greater time to find the objects helpful in sharing the Bible truths. Thinking ahead increases preparation time which improves the presentation. Planning ahead assists in selecting and applying lessons to the theme of the day in our worship services.

C

Continuity of theme. We build anticipation and provide a greater ability for our children to remember the theme of our lessons if we are able to follow through with a theme from week to week. The children know when the children's message is announced what the focus will be. Examples provided in our workbook go on from week to week. When the children come forward, they already have an idea of the type of lesson they will have. They will more likely be able to share what the message was for the previous week since the new lesson is a continuation. You may find it helpful to build on a previous theme if you are working with parts of a whole. Of course, not having the same children in attendance every week might necessitate a brief review.

D

Decide beforehand. This is a simple message of preparation. The greater the preparation the less anxiety we face as the time draws near to share our presentation. Preparation assists greatly in the quality of the presentation. Preparation includes having the needed objects ready and having a clear outline in your mind of the content and direction. Thinking through possible responses to your questions will ease your mind. One caution for over-preparation: we can become robotic in our presentations and unable to respond personally to our children if our message is too structured.

E

Enjoy yourself. What a wonderful privilege is ours to share the news of God's love in Jesus with our young people. We serve as God's messengers. We are God's representatives with opportunities to share God's good news and build relationships with children. Children are a delight to work with. Our joy in service expresses itself in the manner in which we make our presentation. Our joy expresses itself in warmth and acceptance which comes from God.

F

Focus on your young people. The message you share needs to be directed to them. This may sound like a simple idea, yet it is often overlooked. At times messages seem to be directed to the congregation as a whole with the children simply providing a setting for the message. Members of the congregation do listen and learn from the presentation. Sometimes adults express greater interest in the children's lesson than they do in the sermon. Yet our focus is on our children and sharing a message with them.

G

Gospel orientation. While St. Paul taught many different lessons, they are all founded in our relationship to Jesus Christ, as he said in 1 Corinthians 2:2. We believe that Scripture is Christ-centered. As we share our message, such is the theme and foundation of all we have to share, rather than an afterthought. We proclaim the death of Jesus for our sins, and what we share in our lessons is a response to his sacrifice for us.

H

Hand out something. Sending something home with the children has a number of benefits. Most importantly, our young people have something that will assist them in remembering the lesson of the day, and it gives parents the opportunity to discuss with them its significance. They have the ability to share with others the message as they point out what they received. Handing out something is viewed as gift giving. While it may be simple, giving gifts builds relationships. It is important that you are prepared with enough to provide for every child that comes for the lesson. Handing something out seems to encourage young people to come forward for the lesson and participate.

I

Invite them. Inviting and welcoming young people to come forward demonstrates God's open arms welcoming all into his family. So often children as well as adults would like to participate, yet await an invitation. Encouraging and waiting for all to arrive helps all feel comfortable. A parent may be invited to sit with a child during the lesson. In a short time young people will begin to feel comfortable and will come forward on their own.

J

Jobs are interesting. The Christian life is a life of service. Beginning at a young age children are ready and willing to help in some way. They become involved as they handle certain responsibilities that assist in the presentation of the message. If something is distributed, they can take turns handing it out. If a chart or box needs to be moved, they can bring it forward. If something needs to be replaced after the lesson, young hands are eager to help. We set the stage for future involvement through their service at a young age.

K

K-I-S-S-S. These letters are important reminders for making any presentation. Keep It Short, Sweet, and Simple. The elements of the message should relate directly to the theme. Adding other material is only distracting. The simpler the message the more readily it will be remembered and shared with others. The short attention span of younger people necessitates that we get to the point and state it clearly. Simplicity is stressed also in the objects that are used. The more complicated, the more easily something may go wrong.

L

Love them. We love these children and desire to share God's love with them. We do not invite children to come simply to provide a lesson for them. We invite them forward because we care about them and want them to know about God's love in Jesus. Children may not remember their lessons so well over the years in Sunday school, but they do remember their teachers, especially those who brought the love of God to them. It is recommended that a leader serve on a regular basis in sharing the lessons in order to build relationships. A child may demonstrate some hesitancy in coming forward if the face of the teacher changes each week.

M

Moralizing detracts from the Gospel message. Our focus is on the message of God's love in Jesus. Our lives are a response to all that God has done for us in him. We exercise caution as we share our messages so they will not be simple moral lessons based on biblical accounts. Our conclusions do not stress what we should be doing. Our focus remains on what God has done for us and what we can do in response. Our motivation is love of God.

N

Niche in life. As we share our message, we speak to their niche in life. We use illustrations and examples with which they are familiar. We see life through their eyes. We speak in terms of their world and their lives. The more readily they can connect with the illustration, the more significant the message will be to them. We also ask how the message touches their lives. We place them back into life on the playground, in the classroom, at home with brothers and sisters. Will the message make a difference and will they see how to put it into practice?

O

Objects are helpful. Children have a strong visual orientation. We may share stories that they will need to picture in their minds. Having an object before them gives them something tangible with which to connect the lesson. We must exercise caution that the object not overshadow the lesson, but rather introduce the theme. How often we may remember a joke in a sermon, yet miss the message. We introduce the object and then move on to the lesson. At the closing it may serve as a reminder of what was shared.

P

Prayer. Prayer is an important start in our preparations. We turn to the Lord seeking his guidance and the blessings of his Spirit upon us. By submitting ourselves to God's direction he is able more readily to work through us. We also desire our children to grow in their prayer life and so we make it part of our lesson each week. Prayers are simple and can include elements of **A**doration, **C**onfession, **T**hanksgiving, and **S**upplication. Prayers may be offered with the children repeating phrases of our prayers.

Q

Questions involve our children. Questions encourage our children to think, and they promote participation. We see that children are very eager to share. They often amaze us with their knowledge and insights. (We are cautious, though, about asking them about matters of a more personal nature for themselves or their families.) Answers to questions not only assist in the presentation but also provide applications for the message.

R

Regularly include object lessons in worship. Children are not simply the church of the future; they are the church of today. How important it is to share God's Word with them in ways that are readily understood and that are significant for their lives. Having lessons for children at each worship service says that they are important. The lessons become a high point in the service for our young people, as they look forward to their invitation to hear a lesson designed for them.

S

Seat yourself at their level. It is difficult for a child to be seated in the front of the church and look up at the speaker who is standing. Since our focus is on the children, they may be seated on the steps of the chancel with the speaker standing in the aisle. Or the speaker may be seated on the steps and gather the children around. In this way we share a closeness with the children and build stronger relationships.

T

Treat them with respect. Acknowledge them as fellow believers and members of God's church, avoiding a patronizing or superior tone of voice. God often amazes us as to how he can work through them. Their ideas are important.

U

Understand their understanding of God. We bear in mind that the thinking of children is very concrete. Abstract thinking about God, the Trinity, the divinity of Jesus does not arise until later. Children go to God's house and think that the pastor is the one who lives there. They may even wave to the pastor and think they are saying hello to Jesus. Children also form their concepts of God through their relationship with their parents and in their participation in Sunday school and Christian day school. As leaders get to know the children better, we have opportunities to ask them their own views of God. Such a discussion will be most enlightening and helpful in preparing our messages.

V

Use vocabulary appropriate for their age level. We are cautious to use words that are clear for our young people. Certain words that are familiar to church workers sometimes mean nothing to even adult members of the congregation. Using heavy theological terms may lose the listeners. The only exception would be if we are introducing a key word as our main concept.

W

Welcome them. As the young people arrive, we provide words of welcome assuring them that their presence is appreciated. We take just a short time to say hello and begin the relationship-building process. We let them know we care about them and their lives. More often than not they will have something to share.

X

The Greek letter chi stands for Christ. We are reminded that we are not presenting the message on our own. Christ assures us that he is with us always and gives us the gift of the Spirit who will speak to us and through us. We share our message and the Holy Spirit works faith in the hearts of our children.

Y

Yeast makes something happen. Our message begins something that will continue beyond our short time together. We may encourage them to share the message with a friend. After sharing one of our experiences we may encourage conversation with parents. There may be a task they can perform later that day or throughout the week that demonstrates what we have talked about.

Z

Zeal inspires others. We are encouraged to set about our task of sharing God's Word with our young people with enthusiasm. What a wonderful opportunity we have to share the good news of God's love in Jesus with children. We build relationships with them which exhibit the loving relationship that is theirs with God in Jesus. We not only impact their lives, but also their eternity. We share a life-changing message. How exciting to plan and then present God's good news!

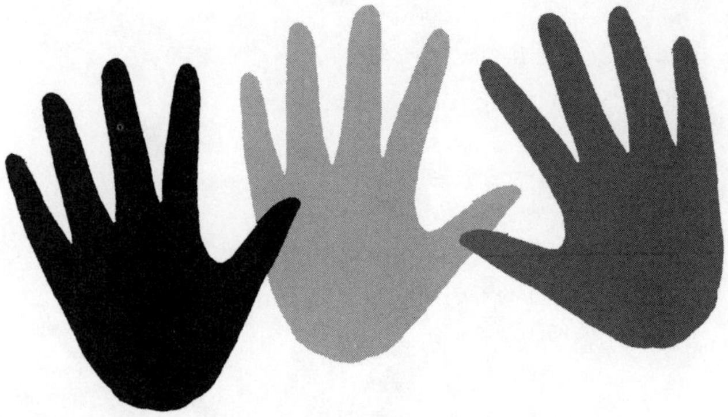

27 Lessons

LABORS of LOVE
Occupations

This series of object lessons focuses on occupations, with each providing a lesson on God's great work of salvation. Each week the leader may show the children a simple object related to each occupation, or, with a little more preparation, the leader could appear in costume.

FARMER
As a farmer plants seeds, we think of the parable of the sower. God plants his Word in our hearts and by his grace it grows.
Suggested Scripture: 1 Peter 1:23

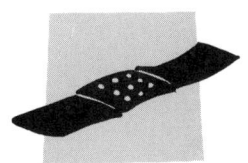

PHYSICIAN
Jesus came as the great physician providing healing not only in body but for our sin-sick souls, as well.
Suggested Scripture: Psalm 103:2-3

CARPENTER
Jesus was known as a carpenter, his trade in Nazareth. He did his greatest work with wood, the wood of the cross.
Suggested Scripture: Mark 6:2-3

CAPTAIN
The Christian life is pictured as involving battle. God is our captain who leads us and from whom we receive directions.
Suggested Scripture: 2 Chronicles 13:12

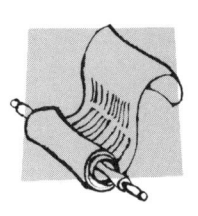

PROPHET
Jesus came as a prophet, God's final prophet. He taught in word and deed. His message was of love taught from the cross.
Suggested Scripture: John 6:14

SERVANT
Jesus is pictured as the suffering servant, the one who came to serve us by bearing our sin.
Suggested Scripture: Isaiah 53:11

PRIEST
Jesus served as a priest in two ways. He offered his own life as a sacrifice for our sins; he prays for us.
Suggested Scripture: Hebrews 7:26-27

JUDGE
Jesus is the judge before whom we must stand and give an accounting. Yet there is no fear, for we know it will be a time of blessings because of his love for us.
Suggested Scripture: 2 Timothy 4:8

SHEPHERD
Jesus is our Good Shepherd who cares for us, leads us to heaven, and sacrificed his own life for our eternal safety.
Suggested Scripture: John 10:14

BUILDER
God is at work building his church. Each of us is an individual stone. We also build up one another.
Suggested Scripture: 1 Corinthians 3:9

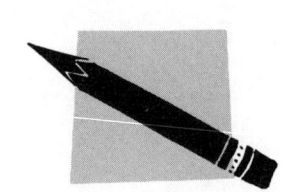

AUTHOR
Jesus is described as the author of our faith. He is also the author of his Word, relying on human writers.
Suggested Scripture: Hebrews 12:2

KING

Jesus is our King who rules in our hearts. He also rules over all for the good of his children. The role of the King was to provide laws for order and protection from evil.
Suggested Scripture: John 18:36-37

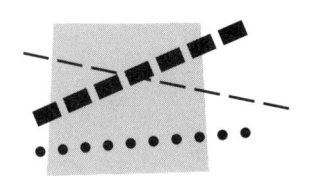

ROAD MAKER

John told us to prepare the way of the Lord. Jesus made the road that gets us to heaven. He himself is that road.
Suggested Scripture: John 14:6

COUNSELOR

The counselor is one who "stands beside" us. He is the wise one who is always ready to listen and to help and guide us.
Suggested Scripture: Isaiah 28:29

WATCHMAN

Jesus keeps watch over us. He stands guard to protect us. His sentinel is continuous.
Suggested Scripture: Psalm 127:1

GARDENER

Jesus is continually at work with us, helping us grow and produce fruit of love and peace.
Suggested Scripture: John 15:1-2

TEACHER

Jesus is our teacher. He is the best teacher who has come from God. Teachers teach in what they say, but also in lives that can be followed.
Suggested Scripture: John 3:2

POTTER
God made us and is continuing to work with us to mold us to be the people he has in mind.
Suggested Scriptures: Job 10:8-9; Genesis 2:7; Isaiah 64:8

GUIDE
God is our guide, leading us on the path of life. Since we are strangers and foreigners in this land, he leads us to our heavenly home.
Suggested Scripture: Psalm 48:14

AMBASSADOR
The ambassador is a representative who lives in a foreign land representing the leader of his own country. We serve as representatives of Jesus as we live in this world (Phil. 3:20; 2 Cor. 5:20). Our true native land is heaven (Eph. 2:19).

ATHLETE
Athletes are those who compete in a contest. To do so they must keep in shape. We have a call to keep our faith in shape that it will serve us well in our lives (1 Cor. 9:25). We run the race and await the prize of heaven (2 Tim. 4:8).

BEGGAR
We are beggars before God who has blessed us bountifully (Lk. 6:20). We remember Jesus who made himself poor that we would be made rich indeed (2 Cor. 8:9).

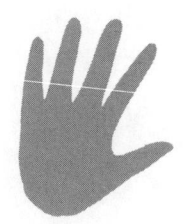

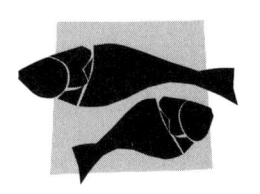

FISHERMAN
We are called to be fishers of men by Jesus (Matt. 4:19). It is important to note that while fishermen catch live fish to their death, Jesus sends us out to catch those who are dead that they may enjoy his life.

HARVESTER
The harvest is a picture Jesus used to speak of souls that are gathered through our mission efforts (Matt. 9:37-38). The harvest is a time of joy and celebration. Such a celebration takes place in heaven as people repent and come to faith (Lk. 15:10).

PEACEMAKER
Peacemakers were sent to other countries to arrange peace. Peace is not simply a matter of a cessation of hostilities, but an establishing of friendship. Since Jesus established peace with God (Lk. 2:14), we have the opportunity to share that message of peace with others (Matt. 5:9).

SOLDIERS
We are engaged in battle (Eph. 6:12). God provides the necessary equipment (Eph. 6:13-17). We are more than conquerors through Christ (Col. 2:15; Rom. 8:37).

STEWARD
The steward is one who manages the property of another, handing out to fellow workers what is needed that they might do their work. All we own belongs to God, and we give to others what they need: the Gospel message. (Eph. 3:2; 1 Cor. 4:1)

STATES
and their Nicknames

50 Lessons

A series of object lessons based on the fifty states is a natural, since it provides enough topics for the entire year. Children's vacations, backgrounds, family ties and affinity for maps connect easily to this subject. The six pages at the end of this section can be reproduced on card stock, cut apart and handed out as take-homes for the children.

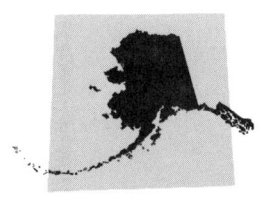

ALASKA, Land of the Midnight Sun
The idea that the sun never goes down reminds us of the eternity of God, no beginning and no ending.
Suggested Scripture: Revelation 22:13

ALABAMA, Heart of Dixie
The human heart is where God's work is done, but God also wants us to love him with our souls and minds as well.
Suggested Scripture: Matthew 22:37

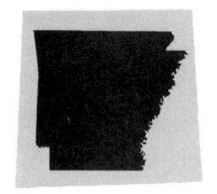

ARKANSAS, Land of Opportunity
Each day we have a new opportunity to serve our Lord. A stewardship theme is present.
Suggested Scripture: Galatians 6:10

ARIZONA, Grand Canyon State
We notice how deep the canyon is, requiring quite a hike. We remember the journey Jesus made to come down from heaven into our world.
Suggested Scripture: Philippians 2:7

CALIFORNIA, The Golden State
We remember three gifts offered to Jesus: gold, frankincense, and myrrh. These are small gifts in contrast to the cost of our salvation.
Suggested Scripture: Matthew 2:11

COLORADO, Centennial State
Since centennial reminds us of 100, we have promises from God of a return of a hundredfold. This serves as a good Labor Day theme.
Suggested Scripture: Matthew 13:23

CONNECTICUT, Constitution State
Since the Constitution governs our lives, we recall the law of God which governs our lives.
Suggested Scripture: Psalm 19:7

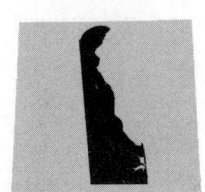

DELAWARE, First State
We are reminded that Jesus is the first and the last, the Alpha and the Omega.
Suggested Scripture: Revelation 22:13

FLORIDA, Sunshine State
We think of the warm sun shining on us and we remember the light of God shining on us, warming our hearts.
Suggested Scripture: Psalm 4:6

GEORGIA, Goober State
Goobers are peanuts. We can focus on the planting of seeds. We plant the seed of the Word.
Suggested Scripture: Luke 8:11

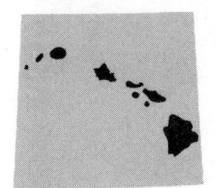

HAWAII, Aloha State
Aloha is a welcome. We think of the welcome arms of God for sinners.
Suggested Scripture: Mark 10:16

IDAHO, Gem State
Gems are very precious like the pearl of great price that Jesus described in a parable.
Suggested Scripture: Matthew 13:45-46

ILLINOIS, Land of Lincoln
The state is remembered for President Lincoln, who lived there long ago. We remember the Holy Land where Jesus lived, and the place where he lives now—our hearts.
Suggested Scripture: John 14:23

INDIANA, Hoosier State
The word "Hoosier" originates from the phrase "Who's here?" The mission hymn reminds us of our response, "Here am I, send me."
Suggested Scripture: Isaiah 6:8

IOWA, Hawkeye State
The state is named after Chief Blackhawk. We think of God's eye watching over us. An Indian Ojo is the eye of God.
Suggested Scripture: Psalm 34:15

KANSAS, Wheat State
Wheat is used for bread. We remember Jesus as the Bread of Life.
Suggested Scripture: John 6:35

KENTUCKY, Blue Grass State
The theme of pasture comes to mind with Jesus leading us to good pastures. This is a good lesson for Good Shepherd Sunday.
Suggested Scripture: Exodus 13:18

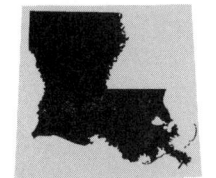

LOUISIANA, Bayou State
Use a play on words and remember that Jesus is "by you."
Suggested Scripture: Matthew 28:20

MAINE, Pine Tree State
Pine wood is a good building material. God is the master builder. We build up one another.
Suggested Scripture: Hebrews 3:3-4

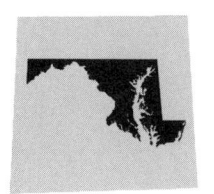

MARYLAND, Free State
We are reminded that we are free from sin, death, and the devil. We are free to serve God in Jesus.
Suggested Scripture: Luke 4:18

MASSACHUSETTS, Bay State
A bay is a partly enclosed body of water with a wide opening to the sea. We find a safe harbor like that in Jesus.
Suggested Scripture: Psalm 27:5

MICHIGAN, Great Lake State
With the lake we have the presence of water. Water reminds us of the waters of baptism. This is a good lesson for Baptism of our Lord Sunday.
Suggested Scripture: John 3:5

MINNESOTA, North Star State
The North Star served as a guide for navigation. We rely on Jesus as our guide.
Suggested Scripture: Psalm 48:14

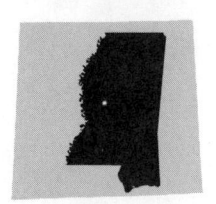

MISSISSIPPI, Magnolia State
The magnolia flower received its name from botanist Pierre Magnol. How did we receive our names? How Jesus received his name is the focus.
Suggested Scripture: Luke 1:31

MISSOURI, Show Me State
Missourians needed to be shown before they would believe, like Thomas. We have faith without sight.
Suggested Scripture: John 20:29

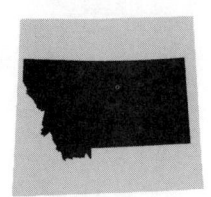

MONTANA, Big Sky Country
With the state so big and people far from one another we remember that our sins are far removed from us as the east is from the west.
Suggested Scripture: Psalm 103:12

NEBRASKA, Cornhusker State
Cornhusking reminds us of the theme of harvesting. This can be a thanksgiving theme or God's harvest at the end of days.
Suggested Scripture: Matthew 13:30

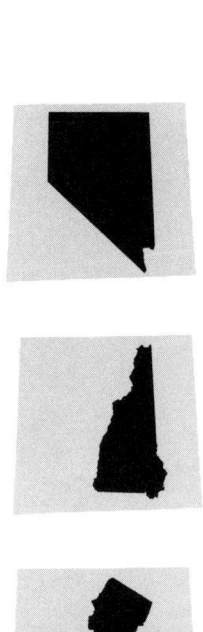

NEVADA, Silver State
The silver reminds us of our treasures from God. We have a stewardship theme presented.
Suggested Scripture: Matthew 22:21

NEW HAMPSHIRE, Granite State
We think of rock. We build on the Rock and are safe in the storms of life.
Suggested Scripture: Matthew 7:24-25

NEW JERSEY, Garden State
Many gardens are mentioned in the Bible. The Garden of Eden or the Garden of Gethsemane can be the focus.
Suggested Scripture: Genesis 2:8

NEW MEXICO, Land of Enchantment
We think of a new heaven and a new earth. The beauty of heaven could be discussed.
Suggested Scripture: Revelation 21:1

NEW YORK, Empire State
We think of God's empire. By faith we belong to God's kingdom. We pray, "Thy Kingdom come." He rules in our hearts.
Suggested Scripture: Matthew 19:14

NORTH CAROLINA, Tarheel State
Thinking of heels we remember God's statement to Satan about Jesus, "He will strike your head, and you will strike his heel."
Suggested Scripture: Genesis 3:15

NORTH DAKOTA, Sioux State
Named after the Siouon language spoken there. We think of our language; our conversation is of heaven.
Suggested Scripture: Colossians 4:6

OHIO, Buckeye State
A buckeye is a nut that looks like the eye of a buck. Our eyes look to God.
Suggested Scripture: Psalm 145:15

OKLAHOMA, Sooner State
Sooners were settlers who were overeager to claim land in Oklahoma and who arrived too soon. God gives us eager hearts to hear his Word and do his will.
Suggested Scripture: Acts 16:14

OREGON, Beaver State
We are busy as beavers, a stewardship theme. We are encouraged to work while it is day.
Suggested Scripture: John 9:4

PENNSYLVANIA, Keystone State
Jesus is described as both the keystone and the cornerstone.
Suggested Scripture: Matthew 21:42

RHODE ISLAND, Little Rhody, Little State
We think of something small, the widow's mite. It's not a matter of size, but of the heart.
Suggested Scripture: Mark 12:42-43

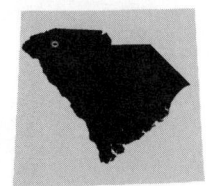

SOUTH CAROLINA, Palmetto State
With the mention of palms we think of Palm Sunday and the honor given to Jesus.
Suggested Scripture: John 12:13

SOUTH DAKOTA, Coyote State
Coyote comes from a word meaning "contemptible" or "sneak." The devil works like this when he tempts us.
Suggested Scripture: 1 Peter 5:8

TENNESSEE, Volunteer State
We can volunteer our time and talents in the Lord's service. This is a good stewardship theme.
Suggested Scripture: Romans 6:13

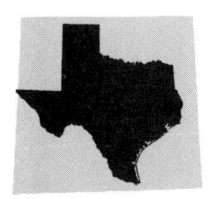

TEXAS, Lone Star State
We think of the special star God provided to guide the wise men. This lesson is perfect for an Epiphany theme.
Suggested Scripture: Matthew 2:2

UTAH, Beehive State
The beehive is a symbol of the church; though one body, it has many members.
Suggested Scripture: Romans 12:4-5

VERMONT, Green Mountain State
The mountain, the Mount of Olives, was a place for Jesus to pray.
Suggested Scripture: Luke 9:28

VIRGINIA, Old Dominion
It was part of the dominion of France. We are part of God's universal dominion.
Suggested Scripture: Colossians 1:13-14

WASHINGTON, Evergreen State
We think of growth in faith and the promises of God that never die, are "evergreen."
Suggested Scripture: Matthew 24:35

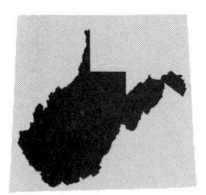

WEST VIRGINIA, Mountain State
On Mount Sinai God gave the covenant to Moses.
Suggested Scripture: Exodus 31:18

WISCONSIN, Badger State
The name refers to mammals that live underground. We think of the death and then resurrection of Jesus.
Suggested Scripture: Ephesians 4:10

WYOMING, Equality State
We are reminded that we were created equal and are equal in God's eyes.
Suggested Scripture: Galatians 3:28

Alabama
Nickname: Heart of Dixie
Meaning: vegetation gatherers
Capital: Montgomery
Bird: Yellowhammer
Tree: Southern Pine
Flower: Camellia
Fish: Largemouth Bass
Rock: Marble
Nut: Pecan

Arkansas
Nickname: Land of Opportunity
Meaning: south wind
Capital: Little Rock
Bird: Mockingbird
Tree: Pine
Flower: Apple Blossom
Gem: Diamond
Insect: Honeybee

Connecticut
Nickname: Constitution State
Meaning: beside a tidal river
Capital: Hartford
Bird: Robin
Tree: White Oak
Flower: Mountain Laurel
Mineral: Garnet
Insect: Praying Mantis
Animal: Sperm Whale

Alaska
Nickname: Land of Midnight Sun
Meaning: "mainland"
Capital: Juneau
Bird: Willow Ptarmigan
Tree: Sitka Spruce
Flower: Forget-me-not
Fish: King Salmon
Sport: Dog Mushing

California
Nickname: The Golden State
Named after a golden island
Capital: Sacramento
Bird: California Valley Quail
Tree: California Redwood
Flower: Golden Poppy
Fish: Golden Trout
Fossil: Saber-tooth Cat
Animal: Grizzly Bear

Delaware
Nickname: The First State
Named after Lord de la Warr
Capital: Dover
Bird: Blue Hen Chicken
Tree: American Holly
Flower: Peach Blossom

Arizona
Nickname: Grand Canyon State
Meaning: little spring
Capital: Phoenix
Bird: Cactus Wren
Tree: Palo Verde
Flower: Saguaro Cactus Blossom
Animal: Ring-tailed Cat

Colorado
Nickname: Centennial State
Meaning: red
Capital: Denver
Bird: Lark Bunting
Tree: Colorado Blue Spruce
Flower: Rocky Mountain
           Columbine
Gem: Aquamarine
Animal: Bighorn Sheep

Florida
Nickname: Sunshine State
Named after Spanish Feast
Capital: Tallahassee
Bird: Mockingbird
Tree: Palmetto Palm
Flower: Orange Blossom
Gem: Moonstone
Animal: Florida Panther
Beverage: Orange Juice

Georgia

Nickname: Peach State

Named after King George II

Capital: Atlanta

Bird: Brown Thrasher

Tree: Live Oak

Flower: Cherokee Rose

Fish: Largemouth Bass

Fossil: Shark Tooth

Insect: Honeybee

Illinois

Nickname: Land of Lincoln

Meaning: warrior

Capital: Springfield

Bird: Cardinal

Tree: White Oak

Flower: Violet

Rock: Fluorite

Animal: White-tailed Deer

Insect: Monarch Butterfly

Kansas

Nickname: Wheat State

Meaning: south wind

Capital: Topeka

Bird: Western Meadowlark

Tree: Cottonwood

Flower: Sunflower

Insect: Honeybee

Animal: American Buffalo

Hawaii

Nickname: Aloha State

Meaning: a small homeland

Capital: Honolulu

Bird: Nene (Hawaiian Goose)

Tree: Kukui (Candlenut)

Flower: Yellow Hibiscus

Colors:
  Oahu — Yellow   Lanai — Yellow
  Kauai – Purple   Hawaii – Red
  Molokai – Green   Nihau – White
  Kahoolawe — Gray   Maui – Pink

Indiana

Nickname: Hoosier State

Meaning: land of Indians

Capital: Indianapolis

Bird: Cardinal

Tree: Tulip Tree

Flower: Peony

Stone: Limestone

Kentucky

Nickname: Blue Grass State

Meaning: plain

Capital: Frankfort

Bird: Cardinal

Tree: Tulip Tree

Flower: Goldenrod

Wild Animal: Gray Squirrel

Idaho

Nickname: Gem State

Capital: Boise

Bird: Mountain Bluebird

Tree: Western White Pine

Flower: Idaho Syringa

Gem: Star Garnet

Horse: Appaloosa

Iowa

Nickname: Hawkeye State

Meaning: one who puts to sleep

Capital: Des Moines

Bird: Eastern Goldfinch

Tree: Oak

Flower: Wild Rose

Rock: Geode

Louisiana

Nickname: Bayou State

Named after Louis XIV

Capital: Baton Rouge

Bird: Eastern Brown Pelican

Tree: Bald Cypress

Flower: Southern Magnolia

Gem: Agate

Insect: Honeybee

Reptile: Alligator

Maine
Nickname: Pine Tree State
Meaning: a mainland
Capital: Augusta
Bird: Chickadee
Tree: Eastern White Pine
Flower: White Pine Cone and Tassel
Fish: Landlocked Salmon
Animal: Moose

Michigan
Nickname: Great Lake State
Meaning: clearing
Capital: Lansing
Bird: Robin
Tree: White Pine
Flower: Apple Blossom
Fish: Trout
Gem: Greenstone
Rock: Petosky Stone

Missouri
Nickname: Show Me State
Meaning: canoe haven
Capital: Jefferson City
Bird: Eastern Bluebird
Tree: Dogwood
Flower: Hawthorn
Mineral: Galena
Rock: Mozarkite

Maryland
Nickname: Free State
Named after Queen Mary
Capital: Annapolis
Bird: Baltimore Oriole
Tree: White Oak
Flower: Black-eyed Susan
Fish: Striped Bass
Sport: Jousting

Minnesota
Nickname: North Star State
Meaning: milky water
Capital: St. Paul
Bird: Common Loon
Tree: Red Pine
Flower: Shadow Lady's Slipper
Rock: Lake Superior Agate
Fish: Walleye

Montana
Nickname: Big Sky Country
Meaning: mountainous
Capital: Helena
Bird: Western Meadowlark
Tree: Ponderosa Pine
Flower: Bitterroot
Fish: Blackspotted Cutthroat Trout

Massachusetts
Nickname: Bay State
Meaning: large hill place
Capital: Boston
Bird: Chickadee
Tree: American Elm
Flower: Mayflower
Insect: Ladybug
Fish: Cod
Beverage: Cranberry Juice

Mississippi
Nickname: Magnolia State
Meaning: large river
Capital: Jackson
Bird: Mockingbird
Tree: Southern Magnolia
Flower: Magnolia
Fossil: Prehistoric Whale
Mammal: White-tailed Deer
Shell: Oyster Shell

Nebraska
Nickname: Cornhusker State
Meaning: broad river
Capital: Lincoln
Bird: Meadowlark
Tree: Cottonwood
Flower: Goldenrod
Fossil: Mammoth
Gem: Blue Agate

Nevada
Nickname: Silver State
Meaning: snowy range
Capital: Carson City
Bird: Mountain Bluebird
Tree: Single Leaf Pinon
Flower: Sagebrush
Fish: Lohonton Cutthroat Trout
Fossil: Ichthyosaur

New Mexico
Nickname: Land of Enchantment
Meaning: place of Mexitili
Capital: Santa Fe
Bird: Road Runner
Tree: Pinon Pine
Flower: Yucca
Fish: Cutthroat Trout
Animal: Black Bear
Rock: Turquoise

North Dakota
Nickname: Sioux State
Meaning: friends
Capital: Bismark
Bird: Western Meadowlark
Tree: American Elm
Flower: Wild Prairie Rose
Fish: Northern Pike
Grass: Western Wheat Grass
Fossil: Teredo Petrified Wood

New Hampshire
Nickname: Granite State
Named after England's Hampshire
Capital: Concord
Bird: Purple Finch
Tree: Paper Birch
Flower: Purple Lilac
Animal: White-tailed Deer
Insect: Ladybug

New York
Nickname: Empire State
Named after Duke of York
Capital: Albany
Bird: Bluebird
Tree: Sugar Maple
Flower: Rose
Fish: Brook or Speckled Trout
Animal: Beaver

Ohio
Nickname: Buckeye State
Meaning: beautiful river
Capital: Columbus
Bird: Cardinal
Tree: Ohio Buckeye
Flower: Scarlet Carnation
Gem: Ohio Flint
Beverage: Tomato Juice

New Jersey
Nickname: Garden State
Named after the Island of Jersey
Capital: Trenton
Bird: Eastern Goldfinch
Tree: Red Oak
Flower: Purple Violet
Animal: Horse
Insect: Honeybee

North Carolina
Nickname: Tarheel State
Named after Charles IX
Capital: Raleigh
Bird: Cardinal
Tree: Pine
Flower: Dogwood
Mammal: Gray Squirrel
Reptile: Turtle

Oklahoma
Nickname: Sooner State
Meaning: red person
Capital: Oklahoma City
Bird: Scissortailed Flycatcher
Tree: Redbud
Flower: Mistletoe
Animal: American Buffalo
Fish: White Bass

Oregon

Nickname: Beaver State
Meaning: storm
Capital: Salem
Bird: Western Meadowlark
Tree: Douglas Fir
Flower: Oregon Grape
Fish: Chinook Salmon
Animal: Beaver
Insect: Swallowtail Butterfly

South Carolina

Nickname: Palmetto State
Named after Charles IX
Capital: Columbia
Bird: Carolina Wren
Tree: Palmetto
Flower: Carolina Jessamine
Animal: White-tailed Deer
Fish: Stripped Bass or Rockfish
Gem: Amethyst

Texas

Nickname: The Lone Star State
Meaning: hello, friend
Capital: Austin
Bird: Mockingbird
Tree: Pecan
Flower: Bluebonnet
Animal: Longhorn
Rock: Topaz

Pennsylvania

Nickname: Keystone State
Meaning: Penn's woods
Capital: Harrisburg
Bird: Ruffed Grouse
Tree: Eastern Hemlock
Flower: Mountain Laurel
Fish: Brook Trout
Insect: Firefly

South Dakota

Nickname: Coyote State
Meaning: friends
Capital: Pierre
Bird: Ringnecked Pheasant
Tree: Black Hills Spruce
Flower: American Pasque
Animal: Coyote
Fish: Walleye
Mineral: Rose Quartz

Utah

Nickname: Beehive State
Meaning: one that is higher up
Capital: Salt Lake City
Bird: California Gull
Tree: Blue Spruce
Flower: Sego Lily
Animal: Elk
Fish: Rainbow Trout
Gem: Topaz

Rhode Island

Nickname: Little Rhody
Meaning: red island
Capital: Providence
Bird: Rhode Island Red Hen
Tree: Red Maple
Flower: Violet
Mineral: Bowenite
Rock: Cumberlandite

Tennessee

Nickname: Volunteer State
Meaning: from Tanasie, a Cherokee village
Capital: Nashville
Bird: Mockingbird
Tree: Tulip Poplar
Flower: Iris
Wild Animal: Raccoon
Insect: Firefly and Ladybug
Rock: Limestone

Vermont

Nickname: Green Mountain State
Meaning: green mountain
Capital: Montpelier
Bird: Hermit Thrush
Tree: Sugar Maple
Flower: Red Clover
Animal: Morgan Horse
Insect: Honeybee
Beverage: Milk

Virginia

Nickname: Old Dominion

Meaning: Virgin Queen

Capital: Richmond

Bird: Cardinal

Tree: American Dogwood

Flower: American Dogwood

Beverage: Milk

Dog: American Foxhound

Shell: Oyster Shell

Wisconsin

Nickname: Badger State

Meaning: grassy place

Capital: Madison

Bird: Robin

Tree: Sugar Maple

Flower: Wood Violet

Fish: Muskellunge

Animal: Badger

Domestic Animal: Dairy Cow

Washington

Nickname: Evergreen State

Named after George Washington

Capital: Olympia

Bird: Willow Goldfinch

Tree: Western Hemlock

Flower: Coast Rhododendron

Fish: Steelhead Trout

Dance: Square Dance

Gem: Petrified Wood

Wyoming

Nickname: Equality State

Meaning: at the big flats

Capital: Cheyenne

Bird: Meadowlark

Tree: Cottonwood

Flower: Indian Paintbrush

Rock: Jade

Fish: Cutthroat Trout

Animal: Buffalo

West Virginia

Nickname: Mountain State

Meaning: Virgin Queen

Capital: Charleston

Bird: Cardinal

Tree: Sugar Maple

Flower: Rhododendron

Animal: Badger

Domestic Animal: Dairy Cow

Fish: Muskellunge

25 Lessons

SIGNS for Our Times

We see many signs along the road to help and guide us. We can often relate these signs to spiritual truths. When children travel, they may be able to remember the message related to each sign.

The leader may wish to enlarge the individual road signs to show the children each week. Or the leader could use markers on foam core to draw a number of intersecting roads, and each week attach a small version of that week's road sign. All the symbols appear on one page at the end of this chapter for easy photocopying or enlargement. Photocopying the page on cardstock to make small cards for handouts is another possibility.

NO PASSING

We do not pass in areas where we cannot see ahead. We cannot see ahead in our lives, but God knows the future and we can trust him.
Suggested Scripture: Jeremiah 29:11

PHONE

The emphasis can be on prayer that is always available, especially in emergencies. God is ready to hear and help.
Suggested Scripture: Psalm 50:15

STOP

We think of Jesus who said "Stop!" to Satan at the time of his temptation. He relied on the power of the Word of God to help him.
Suggested Scripture: Matthew 4:10

COW

We think of sacrifices in Bible times. Sacrifices are no longer needed because Jesus was the final sacrifice offered for sin.
Suggested Scripture: Hebrews 7:27

SCHOOL CHILD
The study of God's Word is important. We learn of Jesus and receive guidance for our lives. This is a lifelong experience.
Suggested Scripture: John 5:39

ROAD SKID
This sign speaks of a dangerous stretch of road. As we face dangerous situations, we are assured there is safety in Jesus.
Suggested Scripture: Psalm 121:3

HIKERS
We see people on a hike walking on a path. We are on the path to heaven laid out for us by God in Jesus.
Suggested Scripture: Psalm 16:11

SEAT BELT
We see the sign that says: It's the law. This is meant for our safety. God gave us his laws in love for our safety and joy.
Suggested Scripture: Psalm 119:2

ROADSIDE TABLE
We see a place where we can stop for a break. It provides relaxation and refreshment. This can be a call to times of meditation and prayer.
Suggested Scripture: Mark 6:31

WRONG WAY
In spite of good intentions we depart from God's ways and ask God for forgiveness, which he offers in Jesus. We commit ourselves to forgiving others in the Lord's Prayer.
Suggested Scripture: Matthew 6:12

DETOUR
Detours help us avoid problem areas. Often in our lives we face detours as God leads us in other directions than we had planned. He means it for our good.
Suggested Scripture: Proverbs 16:9

YIELD
We let other cars go by first. We yield to the will of God as did Jesus.
Suggested Scripture: Luke 22:42

UNDER CONSTRUCTION
The road is being improved. God is constantly at work in us helping us grow and improve.
Suggested Scripture: Ephesians 4:13

ONE WAY
Traffic must go one way. There is only one way to heaven: through our Lord Jesus Christ.
Suggested Scripture: John 14:6

SPEED LIMIT
There is a caution about going too fast. We can go too fast in our lives with too much to do. We get stressed out. We need to slow down and focus on what is important.
Suggested Scripture: Luke 10:42

DIRECTIONS
This helps us know where we should be going. God's Word provides us with direction for our lives.
Suggested Scripture: Psalm 119:105

RAILROAD CROSSING
This sign reminds us of the cross. We can also think of the power of train engines. The Word of God is such a power in our lives.
Suggested Scripture: 1 Corinthians 1:18

CAMPER
A camper is a small temporary home. We think of Jesus who had no home, but lived in poverty for us.
Suggested Scripture: Matthew 8:20

PLAYGROUND
We must be careful, for there are children playing.
We must be care-full, helping others.
Suggested Scripture: Genesis 4:9; 2 Corinthians 1:3-4

HOSPITAL
We think of Jesus as the Great Physician who healed us from sin.
Suggested Scripture: Mark 2:17

FARMER, TRACTOR
The farmer works to produce food. We remember that all good gifts are a result of God's love.
Suggested Scripture: Leviticus 26:4

TENT
These serve as temporary dwellings. Our bodies are earthly tents. They are only temporary until we receive a permanent building from God in heaven.
Suggested Scripture: 2 Corinthians 5:1

DEAD END
This sign reminds us that lots of choices lead to dead ends and it's hard to find our way out. We can turn to Jesus and find our help in him.
Suggested Scripture: Psalm 32:5

CAUTION
We must watch carefully, this sign cautions. We are reminded that we must watch carefully in our spiritual lives, as well, for the devil is at work.
Suggested Scripture: 1 Peter 5:8

PAY TOLL AHEAD
We will never see this sign on the way to heaven. Heaven is a free gift since the payment has already been made by Jesus.
Suggested Scripture: Romans 6:23

39

50 Lessons

Christian Symbols

Christian symbols, which have developed over the ages, offer meaningful subjects for object lessons. This yearlong series links the symbols to the seasons and festivals of the church year, and a weekly schedule is included.

Symbols can be enlarged and colored or pointed out in the sanctuary or church building. They can also be cut from thin wood and painted. A larger board with a series of nails can be used to display the symbols that are described from week to week.

Additional images—for example, denominational logos, congregational symbols, apostles' symbols—might also be included.

Cross
This is the central symbol for Christians. While once it was a sign of shame, it is now a sign of honor, an expression of glory and love of God.
Schedule: Initial session or Lent (Passion Sunday)
Suggested Scripture: Galatians 6:14

Manger
The manger is the symbol for God's gift of his Son, the birth of our Savior. The manger especially denotes his poverty.
Schedule: Sunday after Christmas
Suggested Scripture: Luke 2:7; 2 Corinthians 8:9

Star
The star led the wise men to the Baby of Bethlehem, and symbolizes for us the gift of God's Son for all the world, Jews and Gentiles alike.
Schedule: Epiphany Sunday
Suggested Scripture: Numbers 24:17; Matthew 2:1-2

Shell
The shell is a symbol for baptism, a tool for pouring Jordan River water for our Lord's baptism.
Schedule: Baptism of our Lord
Suggested Scripture: Matthew 28:19; Mark 16:16

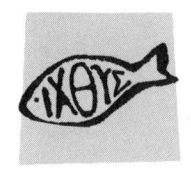

Fish
This is an early symbol for Jesus. The first letters of the phrase "Jesus Christ God's Son Savior" in Greek spell the word fish.
Schedule: Epiphany Season
Suggested Scripture: Matthew 1:21

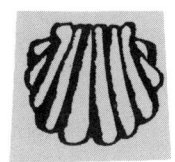

Circle
The circle represents the eternity of God, without beginning and without end.
Schedule: Pentecost Season
Suggested Scripture: Psalm 90:1-2

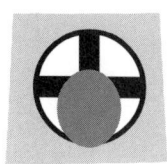

Tri-radiant Nimbus
This halo is sometimes seen around Jesus' head. It stands for the Holy Trinity, and also stresses the divinity of Jesus. The three rays of light are said to represent his divine power.
Schedule: Transfiguration
Suggested Scripture: Matthew 17:2

Torch
This has been a symbol of witnessing for Christ.
Schedule: Epiphany Season or Evangelism Sunday
Suggested Scripture: Matthew 5:16

Heart
The heart is a symbol for love. We remember the love of God shown in Jesus and his call for us to love one another.
Schedule: Valentine's Day
Suggested Scripture: 1 John 4:11

Serpent
This is a symbol for Satan with a focus on temptation.
Schedule: Temptation of our Lord
Suggested Scripture: Genesis 3:1; Matthew 4:1-11

INRI
These letters summarize the sign attached to the cross of Jesus in Latin: Jesus of Nazareth—King of the Jews.
Schedule: Lenten Season
Suggested Scripture: Matthew 27:37

Rooster
A crowing rooster is a warning to Peter regarding his steadfastness of faith and a rebuke in weakness.
Schedule: Lenten Season
Suggested Scripture: Mark 14:72

Basin and Towel
This is a symbol of foot washing. It demonstrates the humility of Jesus and his estimate of true greatness in the kingdom.
Schedule: Lenten Season
Suggested Scripture: John 13:5

Crown of Thorns
This is a symbol of the humiliation and suffering of Jesus. Yet he was a king indeed.
Schedule: Lenten Season
Suggested Scripture: Matthew 27:29

Palm Branch
Palms were considered sacred by people in biblical times. On Palm Sunday or the Sunday of the Passion they were carried as signs of triumphant rejoicing.
Schedule: Lenten Season (Palm Sunday)
Suggested Scripture: John 12:13

Easter Lily

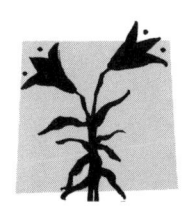

This symbol for Easter stresses immortality—the bulb decays, and from it comes life. The shape appears as trumpets announcing the news of resurrection. It can be applied to the sound of the last trumpet at the resurrection.
Schedule: Easter Season or End of Church Year
Suggested Scripture: 1 Corinthians 15:52

Easter Egg

This Easter symbol is one that emerges. The bright colors denote the joy of new life.
Schedule: Easter Season
Suggested Scripture: Romans 6:4

Sheep

This is a symbol in the Scriptures for God's people. Christ is the Good Shepherd. (It could also be a reference to Jesus as the Lamb of God.)
Schedule: Good Shepherd Sunday
Suggested Scripture: John 10:14 (John 1:29)

Crown

The Scriptures teach that if we are faithful unto death we receive the crown of life. In heaven we rule with Christ.
Schedule: Confirmation Sunday
Suggested Scripture: Revelation 2:10; 2 Timothy 2:12

Dove

The dove signifies the Holy Spirit hovering over the waters at creation and above Jesus at his baptism.
Schedule: Baptism of our Lord or Pentecost
Suggested Scripture: Genesis 1:2; Luke 3:22

Censer
This is a symbol of prayer—as incense moves upward, it was thought to carry the prayers of God's people. May the prayers be pleasing to God as is the smell.
Schedule: Prayer Sunday
Suggested Scripture: Revelation 8:4; Psalm 141:2

Fire
Fire signifies the presence of God speaking to his people as he did to Moses from the burning bush. The tongues of fire at Pentecost are another example.
Schedule: Feast of Pentecost
Suggested Scripture: Exodus 3:2; Acts 2:3

Triangle
This is used as a symbol for God, showing equality and unity of the Father, Son and Holy Spirit.
Schedule: Trinity Sunday
Suggested Scripture: Matthew 28:19

Tables of Law
This is a reminder of the tables of law given by God to Moses.
Schedule: Pentecost Season
Suggested Scripture: Exodus 24:12

Bell
The bell has been used to call people to worship. It is said to symbolize the need to give priority to the things of God. We remember the reason we gather.
Schedule: Pentecost Season
Suggested Scripture: Psalm 86:9

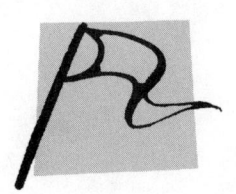

Banner
Banners are symbols of rejoicing and victory. We carry forth the banner of the victory of our Lord.
Schedule: Easter Season
Suggested Scripture: Isaiah 11:10, 12

All-Seeing Eye

The all-seeing (all-knowing) eye of God looks from the symbol of the Trinity and can be seen on American currency. He knows all: our sins and our needs.
Schedule: Pentecost Season
Suggested Scripture: Psalm 139:1-4; Psalm 14:2

Shamrock

This is thought to be the means that St. Patrick used to explain the Trinity in his mission work in Ireland.
Schedule: St. Patrick's Day
Suggested Scripture: Matthew 28:19

Rainbow

This is a symbol of God's promises as given to Noah. The world had war bows, but God's bow is one of love and peace.
Schedule: Pentecost Season
Suggested Scripture: Genesis 9:13

Open Bible

This symbolizes God's Word. It is open and being used. We read it, study it, meditate on it, believe it, and live it.
Schedule: Bible Sunday
Suggested Scripture: Luke 11:28

Sword of the Spirit

The Word of God is described as the sword of the Spirit, part of the armor of God. God's Word is also described as sharper than a two-edged sword.
Schedule: Pentecost Season
Suggested Scripture: Ephesians 6:17; Hebrews 4:2

Lamp
This is a symbol of God's Word drawn from the Psalms. We desire to walk in God's ways, and we know he gives us the will to do this.
Schedule: Pentecost Season
Suggested Scripture: Psalm 119:105

Loaves and Fish
This represents the miracles of Jesus. It is seen also as a reminder of our Lord himself as the Bread of Life.
Schedule: Pentecost Season
Suggested Scripture: Matthew 14:19; John 6:35

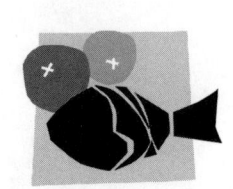

Anchor
This is an ancient symbol for hope used by Christians in hiding in the catacombs. A favorite hymn speaks of this: "Safe I anchor in his grace."
Schedule: Pentecost Season
Suggested Scripture: Hebrews 6:19-20

Cross and Orb
The cross and the world have two significant messages. They remind us that the Gospel is for the world and also that Christ rules over the whole world. He governs all for our good.
Schedule: Epiphany Season or Mission Sunday
Suggested Scripture: Colossians 3:11; Matthew 28:18

Chi-Rho
These are the first two letters in the Greek word for Christ. It reminds us that he is the chosen one.
Schedule: Epiphany Season or Pentecost Season
Suggested Scripture: Matthew 16:16

Beehive
This is an appropriate symbol for the church. It reminds us that the church is a community of those who work together for the benefit of all.
Schedule: Pentecost Season
Suggested Scripture: 1 Corinthians 12:27

Olive Branch

The olive branch is a symbol of peace, harmony, and healing. Olive oil was used in biblical times in ointments for healing.
Schedule: Pentecost Season
Suggested Scripture: John 14:27

Key

This is the symbol used in reference to the keys of the kingdom Jesus gave to his church. We think of our ability to help open the doors of heaven for others by bringing them the forgiveness of sins offered in Jesus.
Schedule: Pentecost Season
Suggested Scripture: Matthew 18:18

Vine and Branches

This symbol is drawn from the words of Christ himself stressing the importance of a close relationship with him. Cut off from Christ we die, yet connected we enjoy his gift of eternal life.
Schedule: Pentecost Season
Suggested Scripture: John 15:5

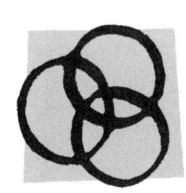

Three Circles

This symbol shows the equality, unity, and co-eternity of the three persons of the Holy Trinity.
Schedule: Trinity Sunday
Suggested Scripture: Romans 11:33

Chalice and Host

This is a symbol for Holy Communion. It also serves as a symbol of the heavenly feast to come.
Schedule: Pentecost Season
Suggested Scripture: Matthew 26:26-28

Cross and Circles

The connected circles are a symbol of two lives joined together in marriage. The cross represents the presence of Christ in the marriage and in the home.
Schedule: Pentecost Season
Suggested Scripture: Matthew 19:5-6

Hand of God

This represents the work of God the Father, stressing not only his act of creation but his acts of preservation as well. It is an open hand from which blessings flow.
Schedule: Pentecost Season
Suggested Scripture: Psalm 145:16

Luther's Seal

The symbol contains many elements. The heart and cross are the image of Christ and are within the Messianic Rose, symbolizing the promise of Jesus coming into full bloom. The circle reminds us of God's eternal word with a backdrop of blue for heaven.
Schedule: Reformation Festival
Suggested Scripture: Isaiah 40:8

Butterfly

This is a symbol of the resurrection. The insect that appears dead leaves its chrysalis and soars upward in new life, just as Jesus leads us to new life.
Schedule: Easter Season
Suggested Scripture: Romans 6:4

Alpha and Omega

These are the first and last letters of the Greek alphabet, emphasizing that Jesus is the first and the last, the beginning and end of all things.
Schedule: Christ the King Sunday
Suggested Scripture: Revelation 1:8

Candle

This is a symbol of Jesus, who is the Light of the world.
Schedule: Advent Season
Suggested Scripture: John 8:12

Harp

The harp is a symbol of worship and God's gift of music. Singing especially is our response of joy to God.
Schedule: Pentecost Season
Suggested Scripture: Revelation 14:2-3

Colors

Each liturgical color has its own symbolism:

Red: blood of martyrs, fire of the Spirit of God

Royal Blue: the coming of the King

Purple: preparation/repentance

Black: death of our Lord

Green: growth in our faith and life

Schedule: beginning or end of church year

What's In a Name?

51 Lessons

This series celebrates God's gifts of individual children to the congregation. Each week the focus of the lesson is on the meaning of the name of one of the children.

Initially, a form is provided for a number of weeks after the service. Parents are invited to return the form indicating their interest in having their children recognized. This becomes a commitment by parents to attend, and this in turn encourages worship attendance.

Once the forms are returned, the leader can research the meaning of the names, choose appropriate Scripture passages, and set a schedule. Numerous name books are available, and a concordance is also a valuable aid. A weekly schedule might coordinate the name meanings with the themes of the worship services throughout the church year.

Use the certificate at the end of this section as an idea for a handout. With fine paper stock, an interesting computer font and a laminating machine, you can create a memorable and very personal handout. Parents should be contacted the week before, letting them know their child will be recognized so they are sure to be present.

Aaron:
Mountain Of Strength
God promised that we can find our strength in him.
Scripture: Exodus 15:2

Adam:
From The Earth
Adam was made from the earth. God has made us all; each one is his special creation.
Scripture: Genesis 2:7

Alicia:
Truthful One
Pilate and Jesus spoke of truth. We shall know the truth in Jesus and the truth shall set us free.
Scripture: Proverbs 12:22b

Alison:
Of Noble Birth
We are born from above, of noble birth, children of the King.
Scripture: Proverbs 31:10

Amanda:
Faithful
God has shown his faithfulness to us despite our sins. May he keep us faithful to him our entire lives.
Scripture: Revelation 2:10

Arlene:
Promise
We have wonderful promises from God to protect us and the promise of heaven with Jesus. Remember some of God's promises —to Noah, Abraham and Sarah, to be with us always.
Scripture: 2 Peter 3:132

Bethany:
House Of Figs
There are important lessons we can learn from the fig tree, lessons which speak of God's Word.
Scripture: Micah 4:4; Matthew 21:18-22; Luke 13:6-9

Bradley:
A Merry Heart
We rejoice in the love and care God provides each and every day.
Scripture: Luke 1:47

Brandon:
A Raven
God provides care for the birds. Ravens were used by God to care for his servant, Elijah.
Scripture: 1 Kings 17:6

Brett:
Gifted
Each person has special gifts given by God. We serve God by making use of these gifts.
Scripture: James 1:17

Carla:
Fully Grown
God desires we mature as his children. He provides his Word, life's experiences, and prayer to help us.
Scripture: James 1:4

Christopher:
Watchful One
We are encouraged to be watchful, especially for the return of Christ.
Scripture: Colossians 4:2

Colin, Nicole:
Victorious One
The victory of Christ over death is our victory as well. We share in the fruit of his resurrection.
Scripture: 1 Corinthians 15:57

Courtney:
Dweller In The Courts
How good it is to dwell in the courts of God's house. We anticipate the courts of heaven.
Scripture: Psalm 84:10

Dana:
Mother
Mothers are special blessings from God. We may think of Mary, the mother of Jesus. We reflect on Mother's Day.
Scripture: Isaiah 66:13

Daniel:
God Is My Judge
At the last day we will be judged by God. We are declared not guilty because of Jesus. He will welcome us into heaven.
Scripture: 1 Samuel 16:7; Colossians 1:22-23

David:
Beloved
We are all loved so much by the Lord that he willingly gave his Son to die for us.
Scripture: Deuteronomy 33:12

Devin:
Poet
We can focus on the Psalms' wonderful poetry written in praise to God. We can speak of how we can bring praise to God in our lives.
Scripture: Psalm 40:3

Doug:
Black Hill
Jesus climbed a black hill to the cross. In his death we have life. It is *Good* Friday.
Scripture: Psalm 121:1-2

Duane:
Blessed One
We are blessed people because of Jesus Christ. Blessed are those who are happy and content in Christ.
Scripture: Psalm 34:8

Emily:
Industrious One
We are called into service for God to use our gifts and talents.
Scripture: Colossians 3:23

Francesca:
Free One
God has granted us freedom in Jesus Christ from sin, death, and the devil. We are free to serve God.
Scripture: John 8:36

George:
Farmer
Farmers grow crops. We think of our lives producing fruit—sharing God's Word, loving our neighbors.
Scripture: James 5:7

Grace:
Grace Of God
Grace is the undeserved love of God in Jesus Christ. This grace is for all.
Scripture: 1 Corinthians 1:4

Hannah:
Kind
Jesus' kindness is seen in the healing he provided. Our kindness is seen in our service to others.
Scripture: Ephesians 4:32

Isabella:
Consecrated To God
Consecrated means to be set apart for special service. God set us apart for lives dedicated to him.
Scripture: 1 Peter 2:9

Jacob:
One Who Overthrows
God has overthrown the power of Satan. We rejoice in this victory and share in its blessings.
Scripture: Genesis 35:15

Jill
Sweetheart
People are pictured as God's sweethearts, those he loves and to whom he is dedicated.
Scripture: Psalm 17:8

Joshua:
God Of Salvation
God did not condemn but has saved us in our Savior Jesus.
Scripture: Isaiah 12:2

Justin:
Upright
Jesus was perfect in every way, avoiding all temptation.
Scripture: Psalm 11:7

Kathleen, Katie:
Pure
The focus can be on the beatitude about being pure in heart. With a clear focus on God we shall indeed see him.
Scripture: Matthew 5:8

Kent:
Radiant
Our lives are radiant as the light and love of Christ shine in us.
Scripture: Psalm 34:5

Kyle:
Handsome
We talk about handsome faces, but God also talks about handsome feet. Are they? Yes! The feet of those who bring the good news and announce God's salvation.
Scripture: Isaiah 52:7

Krystal:
Clear, Sparkling
We can think of the sparkling water of baptism that washes sin away.
Scripture: Revelation 21:11

Landon:
Rough Land
John encourages us to prepare the way of the Lord, making the rough places smooth.
Scripture: Isaiah 40:4

Lee:
Sheltered Place
Jesus is our sheltered place to whom we can go when facing storms in our lives.
Scripture: Psalm 91:1

Luke:
Light
God teaches us that we are the light of the world proclaiming the deeds of God.
Scripture: Matthew 5:14

Marie, Mary:
Bitter
Although Jesus faced bitter trials and betrayals, he did not respond with bitterness; he responded with supreme love.
Scripture: Luke 23:34

Matthew:
Gift Of God
God gives many gifts. The greatest gift of all is our salvation in Jesus Christ.
Scripture: Romans 6:23

Megan:
Mighty One
We think of Jesus who has power over the wind and the waves. We are mighty, too, because of the victory of Christ.
Scripture: Ephesians 6:10

Michael, Mitchell:
One Who Is Like God
We were made in the likeness of God. The likeness was lost in sin, but we have been restored through Jesus Christ.
Scripture: Ephesians 4:24

Nathan:
He Gave
God gave his one and only son that whoever believes in him shall not perish but have eternal life.
Scripture: Matthew 7:7

Neil:
Champion
We think of All Saints Day, the day we remember those who have run the race and have received the prize.
Scripture: 2 Timothy 4:7

Ronald, Ryan:
King
On Christ the King Sunday we remember Christ who came and is coming as our King.
Scripture: Psalm 21:1

RoseAnn:
Graceful Flower
In the Old Testament flowers are connected with rejoicing. We think of the song "Lo, How a Rose is Blooming."
Scripture: Song of Songs 2:12a

Samantha:
Listener
People often do not listen to Jesus. As God's children we do. He also listens to our prayers.
Scripture: 1 Samuel 3:10

Sarah:
Princess
God promises that those who are led by the Spirit of God are children of God. As his children, we are indeed like princes and princesses.
Scripture: Romans 8:14

Shelby:
Sheltered Tower
Old Testament prophets had difficult times, but they were sure of God's care for them.
Scripture: Deuteronomy 33:27a

Tiffany:
Divine Appearance
Jesus' appearance changed at the transfiguration and he became dazzling white. God again announced that this was his Son.
Scripture: Luke 9:29

William:
Protector
We know God is our protector who keeps us safe from sin, death, and the devil.
Scripture: Psalm 32:7

Zachary:
The Lord Has Remembered
While the Lord forgets our sins, he remembers us and saves us. He remembered the thief on the cross.
Scripture: Psalm 25:6

Christopher

WATCHFUL ONE

✠

Devote yourselves to prayer, being watchful and thankful.
Colossians 4:2

14 Lessons

A Church Tour

During the summer months many of the children will go on vacation, traveling throughout the United States. This can be an occasion to go on a trip through the sanctuary. Each week we can take the children to a different location. They are introduced to various items connected with worship and also gain an understanding of their significance.

Baptism
For many of us this is the first place we visit when we come to church for the first time. This is where our life with God begins. This is our entrance into God's family.
Suggested Scripture: Mark 16:16

Altar
Altars were places of sacrifice in Bible times. Sacrifices are no longer needed since Jesus was God's final sacrifice. It is here where we offer our gifts and receive Christ's gift of his body and blood.
Suggested Scripture: Hebrews 10:12, 18

Banners
Banners in history have been signs of victory. A symbol in the church is the Lamb with a banner. Banners help rally the troops in battle.
Suggested Scriptures: 1 Corinthians 15:57 and Revelation 17:14

Pew
A pew is a raised bench. We say "phew" when we rest after working hard. The church is a place where we find rest.
Suggested Scripture: Matthew 11:28-29

Flags
The position of the flags reminds us of the left and right hand of God. The country flag reminds us of God's way of protecting us. The Christian flag speaks of Christ. We have allegiance to both.
Suggested Scripture: Romans 13:1-2

Kneeler
People kneel before a king. When they do, they are ready to receive a blessing. In the rite of confirmation, we kneel to receive his blessing. We receive forgiveness as we kneel for the Lord's Supper.
Suggested Scripture: Psalm 95:6

Chancel
The word chancel means lattice work or a see-through divider. We are reminded that now there is no division between us and God as there was in the Temple.
Suggested Scripture: Ephesians 3:12

Cross
The cross is central to our faith. We can see crosses in every direction in our sanctuaries. We have a constant reminder of Jesus and his death for us.
Suggested Scripture: 1 Corinthians 1:18

Nave
The word nave means ship. This is a symbol of the church taken from Noah's ark. This carried him to safety amidst the flood. We will safely arrive in heaven amid the storms of life.
Suggested Scripture: 1 Peter 3:20-21

Pulpit
The pulpit is the front part of a boat. Jesus preached from a boat. Now from the front of the church God's Word continues today.
Suggested Scripture: Mark 4:1-2a

Aisle
We think of walking down the aisle. This is a reference to marriage. With the church as the Bride of Christ, we think of walking down the aisle as we enter to meet our Bridegroom, Jesus.
Suggested Scripture: Isaiah 54:5

Candles
Candles represent the light of Christ. We also have our little Gospel lights that we allow to shine in our dark world of sin.
Suggested Scriptures: Matthew 4:16 and 5:16

Lectern
The word lectern means to read. We stress the importance of gathering around and reading God's Word as part of our worship experience.
Suggested Scriptures: Luke 24:32 and Romans 15:4

Narthex
The word means box or coffin, which is a symbol of death. We pass through the narthex reminding us that we pass through death into life with God as we come to worship. On our way out of church we pass through death to life beyond.
Suggested Scripture: John 5:24

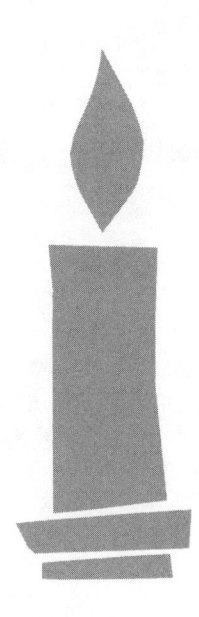

11 Lessons

Tool Box

This series of object lessons focuses on tools used in biblical times. Some of the tools have symbolic meanings; others teach us by the way they are used.

Awl
The awl was used to make markings on wood or stone that was to be cut. We think of how God made his mark on us in baptism.
Suggested Scripture: Revelation 20:4

Ax
The ax is a sign of judgment in the Bible. Yet judgment is not something we fear due to the love of God shown in Jesus. Judgment is a time when we are welcomed into heaven.
Suggested Scripture: Matthew 3:10; Matthew 25:34

Chisel
Chisels are used to make engravings. Engravings in stone last a long time. Job desired that the news of God be engraved and shared with future generations.
Suggested Scripture: Job 19:24-25

Drill
A chest with a hole drilled in it was put next to the altar in the house of the Lord for the people's offerings. Talk about the various offerings children can give to the Lord.
Suggested Scripture: 2 Kings 12:9

Hammer
In the passage the Word of the Lord is like a hammer that breaks rocks into pieces where we can discover gems. The Word of the Lord breaks through the Law showing us our sin, yet displays the treasure of God's grace in the Gospel.
Suggested Scripture: Jeremiah 23:29

Tape Measure

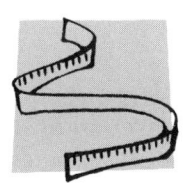

Tape measures vary in length. Some are not long enough. We cannot measure all the blessings God provides as the Scripture shows us.
Suggested Scripture: Job 11:8-9

Nails

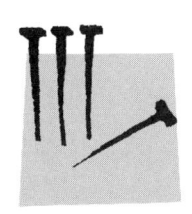

Nails are used to hold things together. We are reminded in the Bible that Jesus is the one who holds all things together. This is true in our lives and relationships.
Suggested Scripture: Colossians 1:17

Ruler (straight edge)

When we want to make a straight line, we rely on the straight edge. We ask God to help us walk a straight path.
Suggested Scripture: Psalm 119:9

Saw

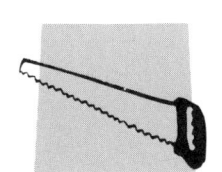

The saying goes: Measure twice, cut once. If we do not measure carefully, we may cut in the wrong place and ruin our work. We can ruin a lifetime apart from God.
Suggested Scripture: Proverbs 10:27

Sand Paper

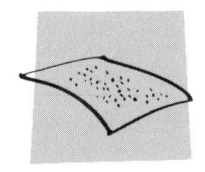

In biblical times pieces of limestone were used to make things smooth. God encourages us to make the road smooth so that he can come into our hearts and lives.
Suggested Scripture: Luke 3:5

Square

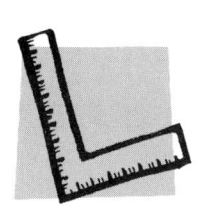

A square is used so that the building project isn't crooked, but straight with corners at right angles. We ask God to make our words and conduct match our faith.
Suggested Scripture: Proverbs 8:8

Hiking with the Psalms

27 Lessons

This series of object lessons takes our children on a journey with the Book of Psalms and its beautiful imagery providing the Scripture references. You will find an example of a map with symbols at the end of this section. Your presentation might be enhanced with a large map like this on which to mark your progress each week. You might enjoy mapping an actual area near your church or creating a totally imaginary one.

Compass

Our first stop introduces us to the theme of a hike. We are going on a hike and one thing we might need is a compass. We are also on a journey in our lives headed to heaven. What compass does God provide? (His Word)
Suggested Scripture: Psalm 119:105

Trail Markers

Often hiking trails are cut through the woods and signs are posted to keep us on the trail. God laid out a trail for our lives, and we follow the paths he set for us. What an adventure!
Suggested Scripture: Psalm 25:4-5

Hiking

In days gone by explorers relied on guides to take them into unfamiliar areas. The guides knew the way and provided help along the way. God serves as the guide in our lives and protects us on our hiking adventures as well as every day of our lives.
Suggested Scripture: Psalm 48:14

East

Along the right side of the map we come to the "E" which designates east from west. West is on the far side. We are reminded that God has removed our sins so far from us as the east is from the west.
Suggested Scripture: Psalm 103:12

Stone Wall

We come across obstacles on our hike. One may be an old stone wall that we will have to climb over. God is with us and helps us get over obstacles in our lives.
Suggested Scripture: Psalm 18:29

Picnic Area

Hiking requires energy, so it's important to take a lunch break in order to go on. God is the source of the food that is provided daily for our good.
Suggested Scripture: Psalm 145:15-16

Mountains

We look about on our hike and see mountains all around us. They are great and majestic. In such a way the love of the Lord surrounds us and protects us.
Suggested Scripture: Psalm 125:2

Peak

We are at the highest point in our travels when at the summit. We reach new heights in life because of the love of God in Jesus.
Suggested Scripture: Psalm 18:33

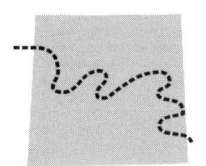

Winding Path

Winding trails, rocky ground, steep climbing make the journey difficult. There may be difficult times in our lives, but we are assured that God is with us and will lead us through them to safety.
Suggested Scripture: Psalm 23:4

Scenic Lookout
The stop on our hike gives us an opportunity to look out and see the beauty and grandeur of God's creation. Did you bring a camera?
Suggested Scripture: Psalm 148:7-13

North Arrow
We carry a compass that points north. It can be trusted to help us on our journey. God's Word can be trusted to serve as our guide.
Suggested Scripture: Psalm 18:30

Shelter
Storms arise and how good it is to have a shelter where we can find refuge. God is our shelter to whom we can go, safe from sin and storms of life.
Suggested Scripture: Psalm 55:8

Lake
The lake is large and can be fierce. Yet God is in charge and has control over the wind and waves.
Suggested Scripture: Psalm 65:7

Lighthouse
The lighthouse helps us know where we are and where we are going so we can avoid danger. The Lord is our light.
Suggested Scripture: Psalm 78:14

River
The river is a place where animals find refreshment. God is the source of refreshment for our lives.
Suggested Scripture: Psalm 42:1

Recycling

God has entrusted his earth to us, and we respond with good stewardship, recycling regularly. It's a good symbol for our lives as well, for God renews us daily as we recall our baptisms.
Suggested Scripture: Psalm 51:10

Drinking Water

Water cleanses and refreshes weary hikers. God's living water restores our souls.
Suggested Scripture: Psalm 23:2-3

Swimming

When we are in danger in the water, we have lifeguards that rescue us. Jesus rescued us from our sins.
Suggested Scripture: Psalm 18:16

Medical Facility

We can rely on Jesus to help us in times of sickness. He is the Great Physician who saved us from the sickness of sin.
Suggested Scripture: Psalm 103:3

Information

If we're lost and need direction, if we don't know which way to turn, God provides for us—through prayer, through his Word, through loving friends and family.
Suggested Scripture: Psalm 119:33-35

Litter Receptacle

We have God's assurance that we are never throw-aways. In his enormous love he picks us up and gives us new beginnings daily.
Suggested Scripture: Psalm 51:1-2

Marshland
You can get stuck in marshland if you are not careful. When life's problems and sin overwhelm us we know we are safe in Jesus.
Suggested Scripture: Psalm 40:2

Campfire
The campfire is a place to gather for singing, togetherness and evening devotions. Each evening we can thank God for his care of us all through the day.
Suggested Scripture: Psalm 18:1-2

Shower
It feels good to get cleaned up. How good it is to know that Jesus washes away the dirt of sin.
Suggested Scripture: Psalm 51:2

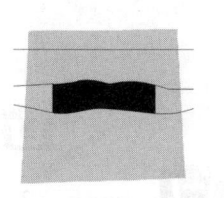

Rapids
It is easy to get swept away and lose our way in life. God is the one who rescues us when we get swept away.
Suggested Scripture: Psalm 42:7

Fishing
When we're camping, fishing provides both fun and food for us. In our life journey God gives us opportunities for fun and sport and provides for our essential daily needs as well.
Suggested Scripture: Psalm 104:24-26

Cemetery
While the graveyard may be the last stop on our journey, it is never the last stop for the child of God. It is a new beginning of life in heaven.
Suggested Scripture: Psalm 49:15

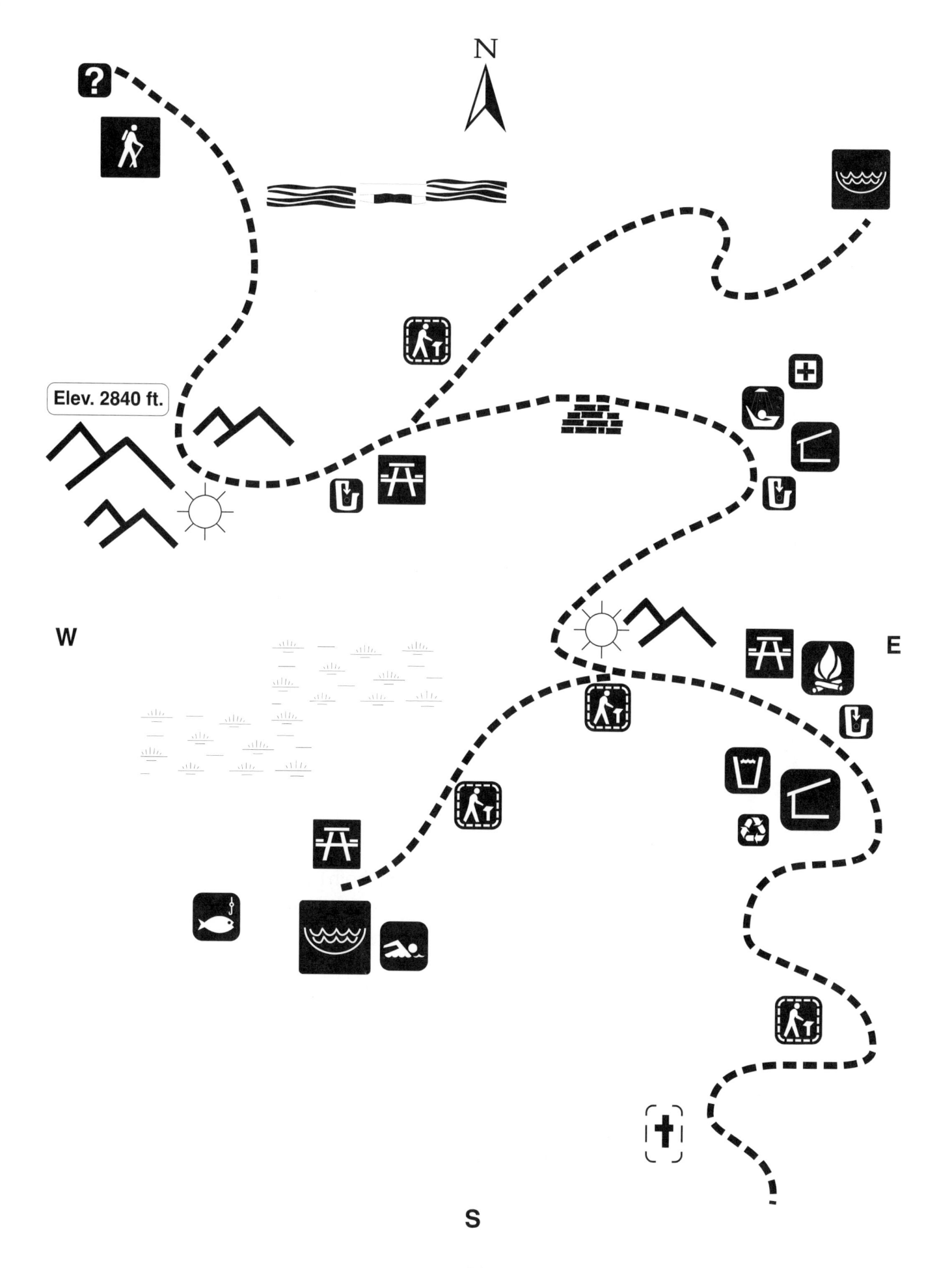

N

W   E

S

Elev. 2840 ft.

71